THE SUN
ITS SPOTS AND FLARES

Astronomy Book for Beginners
Children's Astronomy Books

Speedy Publishing LLC
40 E. Main St. #1156
Newark, DE 19711
www.speedypublishing.com

Copyright 2017

In this book, we're going to cover interesting facts about the spots and solar flares on our Sun. So, let's get right to it!

The Sun is about 93 million miles away from the Earth, but when you see it in the sky it's very bright. In fact, it's so bright that you should never fix your eyes on it, because it can damage your eyesight. Astronomers use special types of telescopes to view the Sun and its interesting features.

WHAT IS THE SUN?

The Sun wasn't always a part of our universe. It was "born" from a huge cloud of gaseous dust about 5 billion years ago. Over many millions of years, the dust and gas began to contract, which generated a lot of pressure and very intense heat.

The Sun kept rising and rising in temperature. When it reached about 1 million degrees Fahrenheit, then its insides ignited, which caused nuclear fusion to begin. Once this happened, the Sun was able to produce its own light as well as heat and energy from its own processes.

Since prehistoric times, people have looked up at the Sun and marveled at its brightness and power. It was worshipped by many ancient tribes. Then, as science emerged, astronomers in the 16th as well as 17th centuries like Galileo Galilei and Isaac Newton started to research the Sun.

They learned that the intense gravity of the Sun caused the planets and other objects in Solar System to revolve around it. In 1905, Albert Einstein proposed his famous formula $E = mc2$, which means that energy is the same as the mass of an object multiplied by the speed of light to the 2nd power.

The formula $E = mc^2$ led to an understanding of how the Sun was able to continuously produce so much intense energy. Building on Einstein's work, Arthur Eddington described

how the pressures at the Sun's center could create nuclear reactions from its gases of hydrogen and helium, producing intense energy and heat.

Solar Probe

Since the late 1950s, unmanned space spacecraft have taken in data about the Sun as well as its sunspots, flares, and wind. There's still a lot to learn about this yellow dwarf star that takes up 99.8% of the mass of our Solar System. Even though the Sun is an average-sized star in the Universe, it's vital to all life on Earth.

The core of the Sun is intensely hot. Its temperature is millions of degrees. Through a process called thermonuclear fusion, the Sun changes hydrogen into another gas called helium.

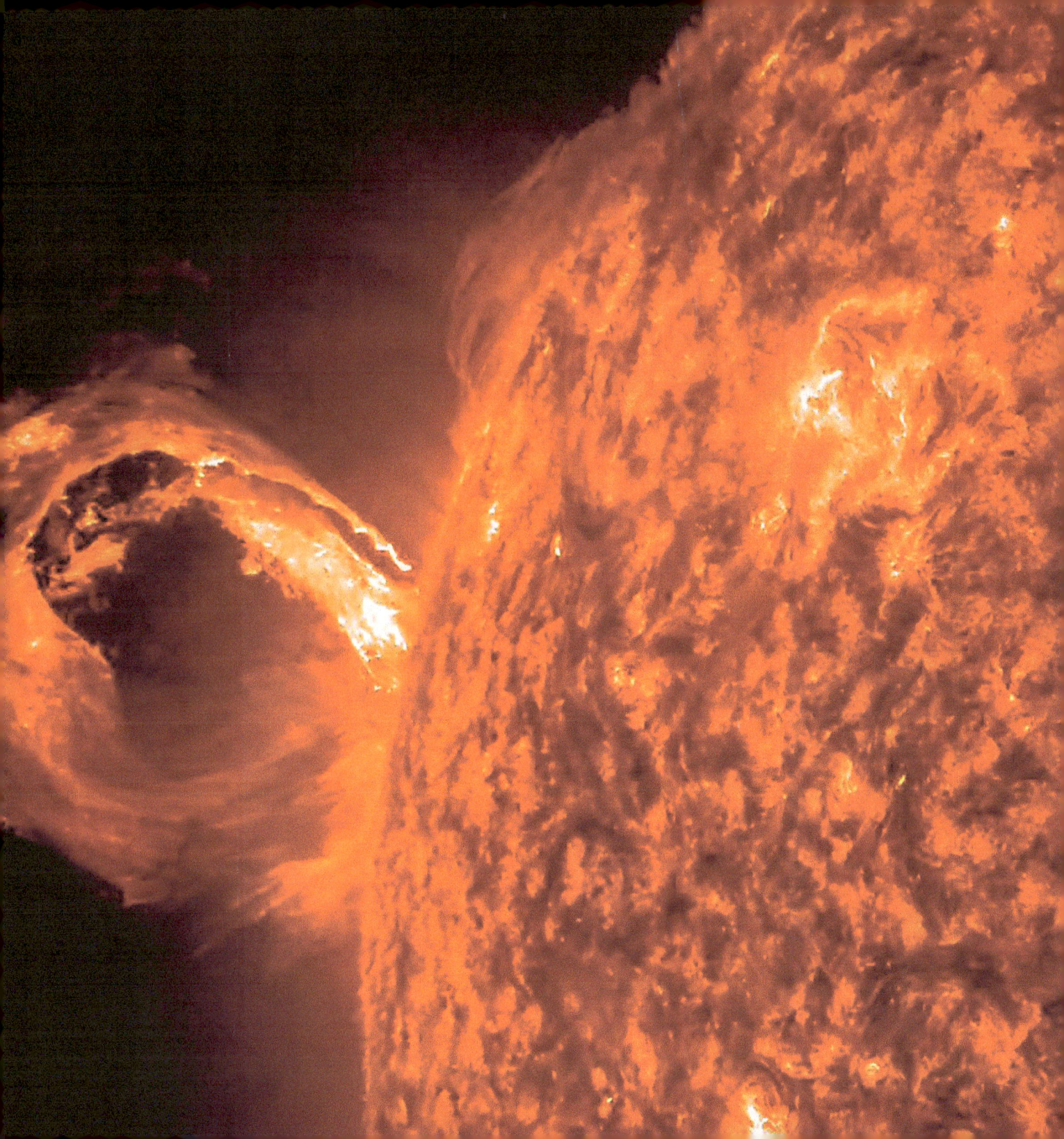

This happens at the core of the Sun and these powerful reactions cause light, heat, and energy to travel outward through our Solar System and the universe. Stars like the Sun "burn" fuel but not in the way that fires on Earth do.

WHAT IS CONVECTION?

If you have several floors in your house, you may have noticed that it's cooler in the basement and much warmer in the attic. The same process happens inside a star. The hot gases rise and cool gases fall. The process continues to repeat in a cycle. A pot of boiling water works this way too. These streams of motion that travel in circular patterns from hot to cold to hot to cold are called convection.

Gases near the Sun's core get heated. Then these gases rise to the surface. Eventually they become a cooler temperature than they were before and they start to sink into the core again, only to repeat the cycle over and over.

A single atom will take millions of years just to go through this cycle one complete turn. The temperature on the outside of the Sun is about 10,000 degrees Fahrenheit, but the inner core is much, much hotter!

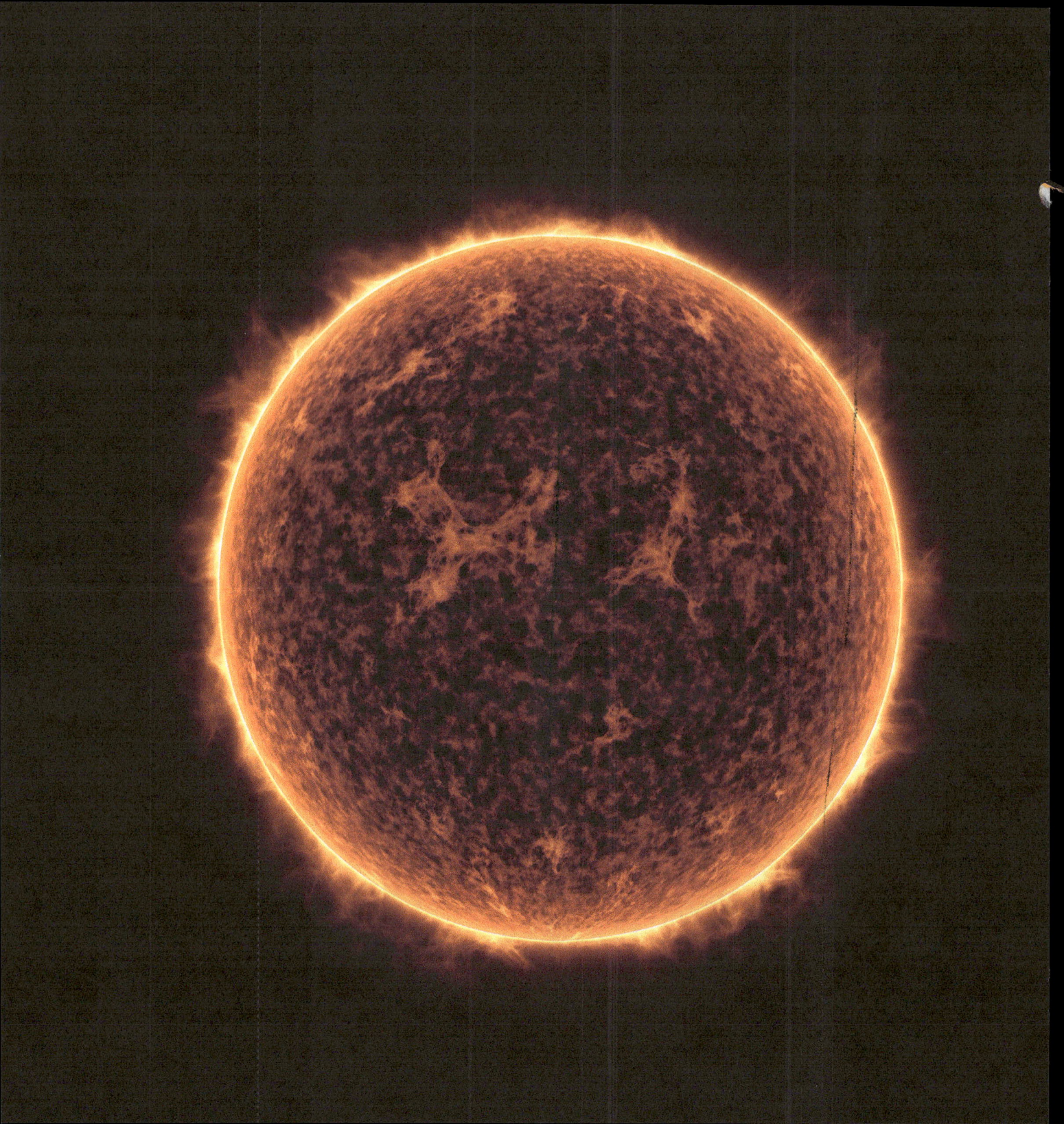

WHAT ARE SUNSPOTS?

The outside surface of the Sun is called the photosphere. The photosphere radiates both heat and light. Sometimes darker areas show up on its surface. These areas are called sunspots. The activity of powerful magnetic energy inside the Sun causes sunspots although scientists are not sure exactly why.

First seen by Chinese astronomers in 364 BC, sunspots show up as darker areas on the Sun's surface. They are cooler in temperature than the surrounding photosphere. Of course, nothing on the surface of the Sun is cool! The temperature of the photosphere is 5,800 degrees Kelvin, but in comparison the sunspots are cooler. They are only 3,800 degrees Kelvin.

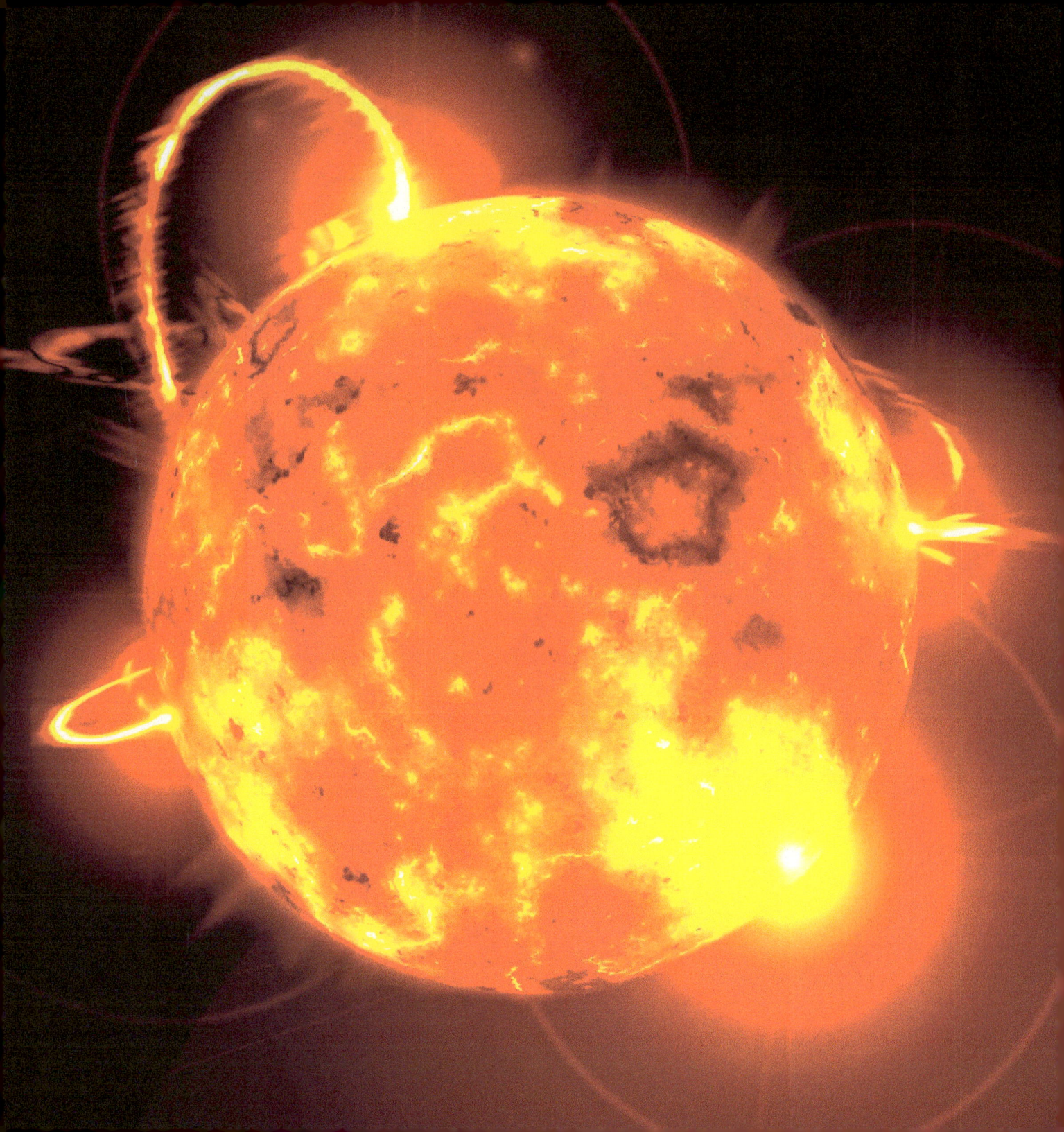

Sunspots, which often appear in pairs, don't stay in one place. Instead, they travel slowly across the Sun's surface and change size as they're moving. Sunspots are all different sizes, from ten thousand miles wide to one hundred thousand miles wide! Sunspots appear on the Sun's surface based on a cycle.

There are always more sunspots during the 11th year of the cycle, which is called the Saros Cycle. The 11th year of the cycle is called solar maximum or solar max. Large solar flares happen during solar maximum.

The forces of gravity are stronger in sunspots than in other areas of the Sun's surface. When the energy from sunspots is emitted, solar flares and huge solar storms called coronal mass ejections occur.

WHAT IS SOLAR WIND?

When we talk about solar wind, we're not talking about anything that's similar to wind on Earth. In fact, we're not talking about air at all. The Sun is a huge mass of constantly moving gas. The huge amounts of energy that come off its surface send a steady stream of charged particles that leave the photosphere and travel out in every direction. This solar wind travels throughout our Solar System.

The stream of particles from the solar wind varies in intensity depending on how active the Sun's surface is. Solar wind would do a lot of damage on Earth if we were not protected by our magnetic field. Earth's magnetic field acts like a "force field" to keep the solar wind from causing damage to our atmosphere. The Sun loses billions of tons of mass hourly from solar wind. Despite the magnetic field, some particles come through the Earth's atmosphere and pass right through our bodies without our realizing it!

The area around the sun where the winds are forceful enough to "blow" outward is called the heliosphere after the Ancient Greek god of the Sun, called Helios. Eventually the winds reach out far enough to where the Sun's force isn't pushing them anymore and they begin to intermix with other gases and particles in space. This matter is called the interstellar medium and it includes gases of different forms as well as cosmic rays and dust.

Aurora Borealis in Norway

The beautiful northern lights, also called *"aurora borealis"* happens when the solar wind collides with the atmosphere of the Earth.

WHAT ARE SOLAR FLARES?

Even though they are actually quite bright, sunspots appear darker then the surface of the Sun and solar flares appear brighter than its other surface. Solar flares are enormous bursts of energy that are emitted outward from the Sun's surface.

They give out a huge amount of electro-magnetic radiation in the form of both X-rays as well as gamma rays. Just one solar flare can have the same amount of energy as one million nuclear explosions going off simultaneously.

In fact, the very intensely charged energy particles emitted from a solar flare travel to Earth within minutes. They sometimes cause damage to satellites and also cause problems for radio signals.

Coronal Mass Ejections, called CME for short, often follow a solar flare. A CME is plasma that's ejected from the Sun's intensely hot surface.

FASCINATING FACTS ABOUT THE SUN

Solar flares can have temperatures up to 24 million degrees Fahrenheit. They spew out thousands of miles outward from the Sun's surface.

Lord Richard C. Carrington was the first astronomer to ever witness a solar flare in 1859.

It was recently discovered that solar flares can sometimes cause sunquakes, which are intense seismic events that are similar to earthquakes on Earth. They release energy that is roughly 40,000 times more intense than the energy released during the San Francisco earthquake of 1906.

San Francisco Earthquake 1906

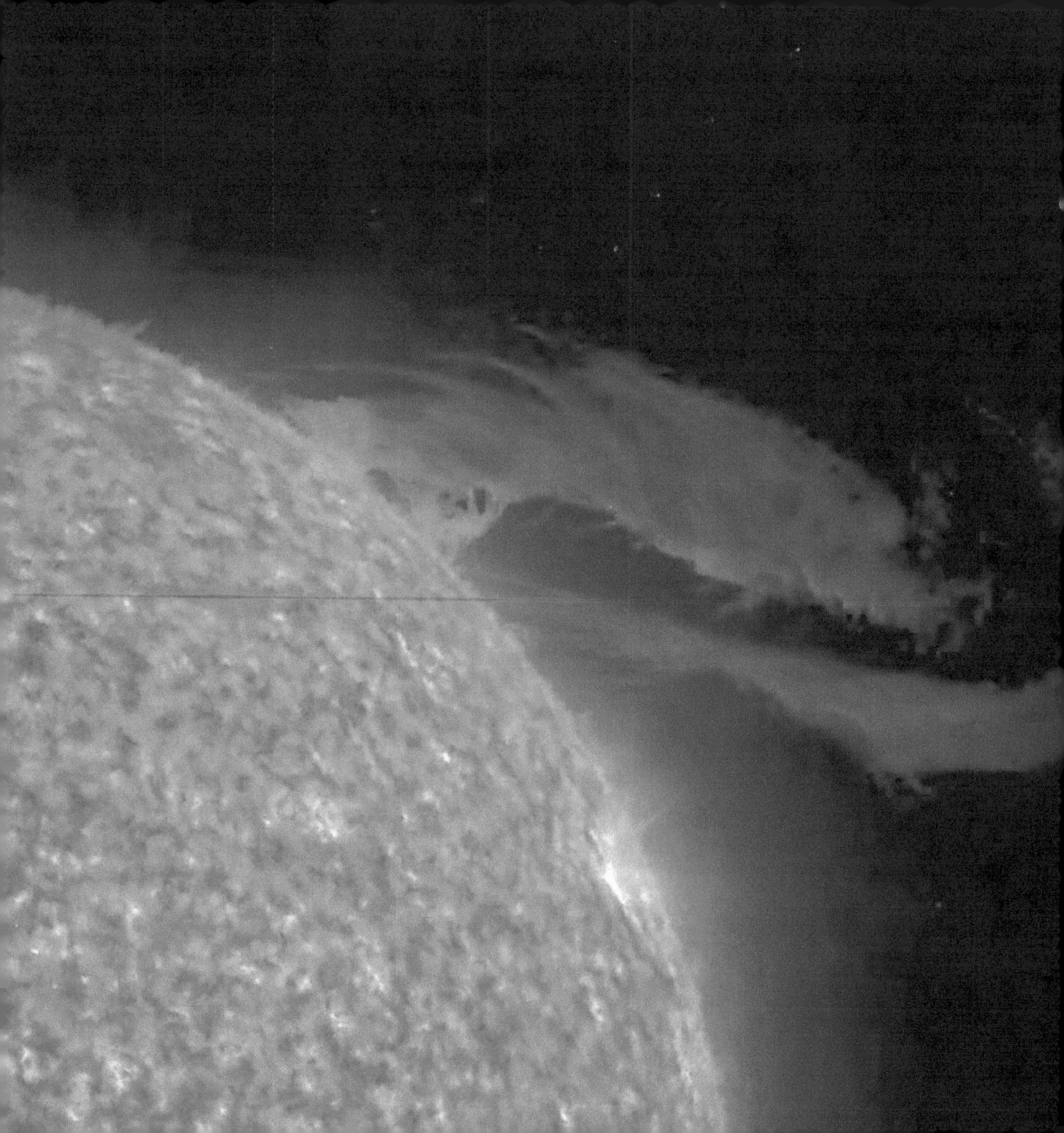

A solar prominence, also called a filament, is a huge archway-shaped gas that bursts out from the Sun's surface. A prominence can extend thousands of miles into space. Prominences are held into their position by intense magnetic fields. They can stay on the surface for months at a time.

A coronal mass ejection can release an amount of plasma equivalent to 220 billion pounds.

In March of 1989, a huge coronal mass ejection created a magnetic storm in the atmosphere of the Earth. A large power station in Canada went down as a result.

During peak times, there can be as many as 20 solar flares daily and as many as 100 solar flares weekly.

Awesome! Now you know a lot more about solar flares and spots. You can find more Astronomy books from Baby Professor by searching the website of your favorite book retailer.

Visit

BABY PROFESSOR
EDUCATION KIDS

www.BabyProfessorBooks.com

to download Free Baby Professor eBooks
and view our catalog of new and exciting
Children's Books